MW00824033

High Voice
TREASURY
Contemporary and Traditional Favorites

Arranged by

Lloyd Larson

Compiled by Ken Bible and John Mathias

Cover design by Ted Ferguson
Music Typesetting by Lyndell Leatherman

Lillenas *PUBLISHING COMPANY*

KANSAS CITY, MO 64141

How Beautiful

T.P.

TWILA PARIS
Arr. by Lloyd Larson

4

beau - ti - ful,_____ how_____

beau - ti - ful,_____ how_____

3rd time to Coda

beau - ti - ful_____ is the bod-y of

8

I Stand in Awe

M.A.

MARK ALTROGGE
Arr. by Lloyd Larson

You are beau-ti-ful be-yond de-scrip-tion,_____ too

mar - vel - ous for___ words, Too won-der-ful for com - pre -

12

Shine on Us

M.W.S. and D.S.

MICHAEL W. SMITH and DEBORAH SMITH

Flowing, expressively

1. Lord, let Your light, light _ of Your
2. Lord, let Your grace, grace _ from Your

face shine _ on _ us.
hand fall _ on _ us.

Lord, let Your light, light from Your
Lord, let Your grace, grace from Your

face shine on us That
hand fall on us That

we may be saved, that
we may be saved, that

16

we may have life To find our
we may have life To find our

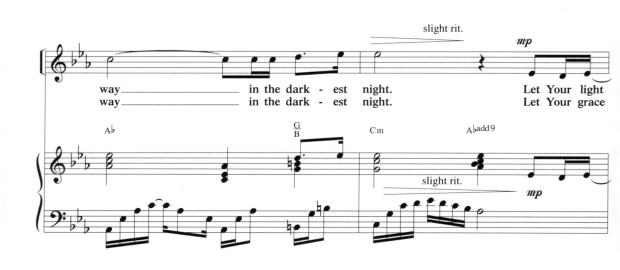

way in the dark - est night. Let Your light
way in the dark - est night. Let Your grace

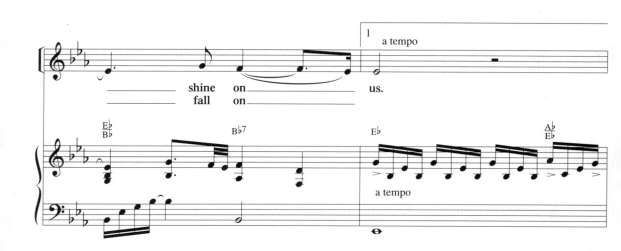

shine on us.
fall on

Crucified with Christ

R.P., D.P., D.K., and D.C.

RANDY PHILLIPS, DENISE PHILLIPS,
DON KOCH, and DAVE CLARK

Arr. by Lloyd Larson

give, For it's not my strength but His._____ There's no

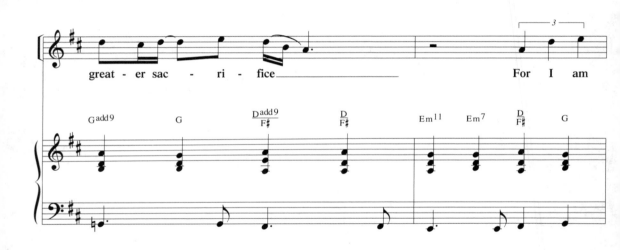

great - er sac - ri - fice_____ For I am

cru - ci - fied___ with Christ_____ and yet I

live!   2. As I   live!

And I will of - fer all___ I   have   so that His

cross is not___ in vain;_____   For I've found to live___ is

28

We Trust in the Name of the Lord Our God

S.C.C.

STEVEN CURTIS CHAPMAN

Driving, with energy

1. Some trust in chariots; We trust in the name of the Lord our God. Some trust in horses; We
2. Some trust in the work they do; We trust in the name of the Lord our God. 'Cause by His grace all the work is thro.' We

30

32

33

Teach Me to Love

S.G., L.H., and P.N.

STEVE GREEN, LARNELLE HARRIS, and PHIL NAISH

But love I can - not find_____ a - lone._____
We need to learn_____ to love_____ a - gain._____

Lord, teach me to love._____ Show me how_____ to care____ for oth-

- ers. Cause my soul_____ to burn with - in for the fel-

40

O Men of God, Arise!

J. M., S. G., and D. H.

JON MOHR, STEVE GREEN, and DAVID HAMILTON
Arr. by Lloyd Larson

men of God,____ a-rise! A-wake from slum-ber's night; Shake
men of God,____ a-rise! Take up your sword and shield. Your

off sin's drow-si-ness and rouse your-self____ to fight.
foe has no de-fense a-gainst the pow'r____ they wield.

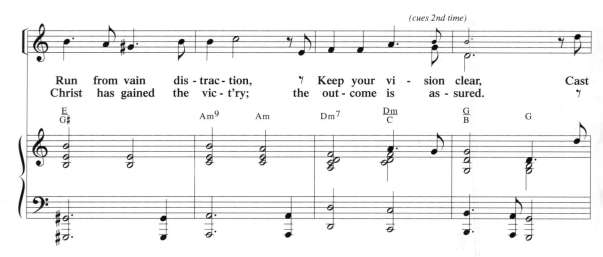

42

(cues 2nd time)

Run from vain dis-trac-tion, Keep your vi-sion clear, Cast
Christ has gained the vic-t'ry; the out-come is as-sured.

out all flesh-ly stow-a-ways, Re-fuse to har-bor fear.
Sa-tan is de-feat-ed by the pow-er of God's Word.

Lift up the cup of ho-li-ness;__ Drink long and take your__

fill.   O   men   of God, a-rise—————————   To   car - ry out,———   to

car - ry out————————   God's   will.

Begin steady tempo

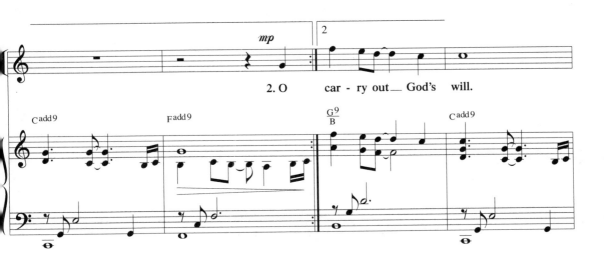

2. O   car - ry out—— God's   will.

3. O men of God,____ a - rise! And face the east - ern

skies, For Christ will soon____ de - scend with

light - ning in____ His eyes. Then our an - cient foe, long

van - quished, will___ meet his right - ful end, And

sin's dark night of ter - ror will nev - er fall a -

gain.___ Lift up the cup of

46

The Great Divide

G.C. and M.H.

GRANT CUNNINGHAM and MATT HUESMAN
Arr. by Lloyd Larson

With strength

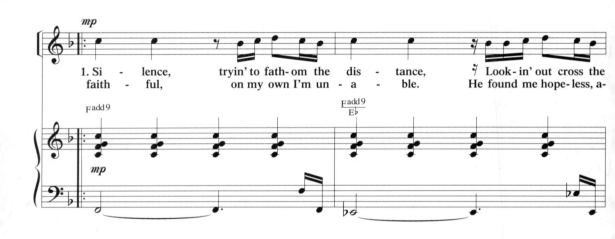

1. Si - lence, tryin' to fath-om the dis - tance, Look-in' out cross the
faith - ful, on my own I'm un - a - ble. He found me hope-less, a-

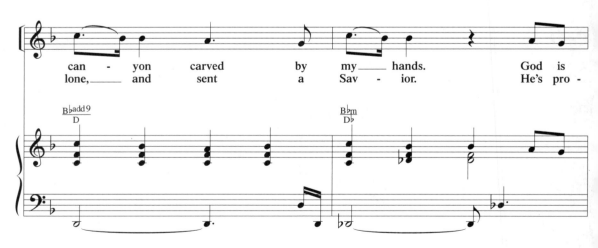

can - yon carved by my ___ hands. God is
lone, ___ and sent a Sav - ior. He's pro -

cross   to bridge the great di - vide.

2. God is   cross   to _ bridge the great di -

vide. The cross that cost_____ my Lord   His life has giv-en me

52

53

love is___ deep,___ His love is___ wide;___ There's a

cross___ to bridge the great di - vide. There's a

cross___ to bridge the great di - vide.

Go Light Your World

C.R.

CHRIS RICE

With assurance

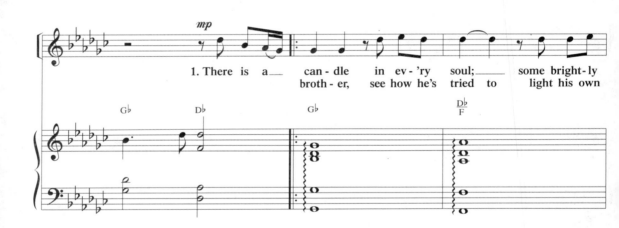

1. There is a_ can - dle in ev - 'ry soul;_ some bright - ly
broth - er, see how he's tried to light his own

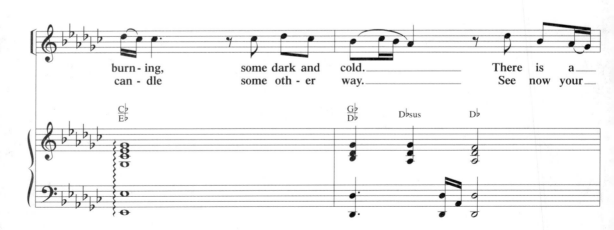

burn - ing, some dark and cold._____ There is a_
can - dle some oth - er way._____ See now your_

56

mp
world.
3. We are a
D
Cadd9/E
D/F♯
fam - 'ly whose hearts are blaz - ing, so let's raise our
G
mp
D/F♯
can - dles and light up the sky! Praying to our
C/E
G/D
D
Cadd9/E
mf
Fa - ther, in the name of Je - sus, make us a
G
mf
D/F♯
G
Gadd9/B

58

60

God Will Make a Way

D.M.

DON MOEN
Arr. by Lloyd Larson

Gently, with some movement

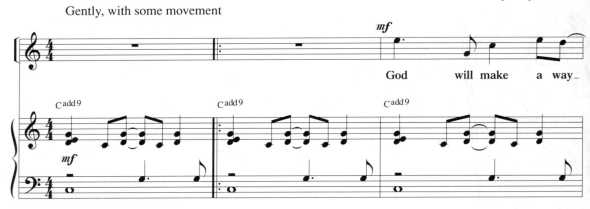

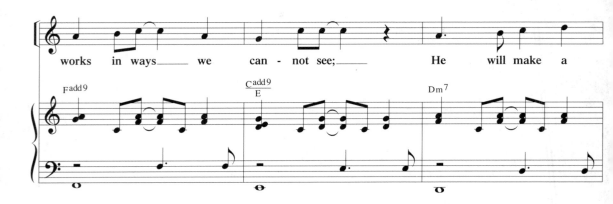

62

64

Thank You

R.B.

RAY BOLTZ

I dreamed I went to heav- en; you were there with me. We

walked up - on the streets of gold be - side the crys - tal sea. We

68

70

He Loved Me with a Cross

J.L. and S.C.S.

JOEL LINDSEY and SUE C. SMITH

74

76

78

The Time Is Now

T.P.

TWILA PARIS
Arr. by Lloyd Larson

We won - der what be - came___ of E - den, while we
There is a vi - sion that___ is bright - er, and___

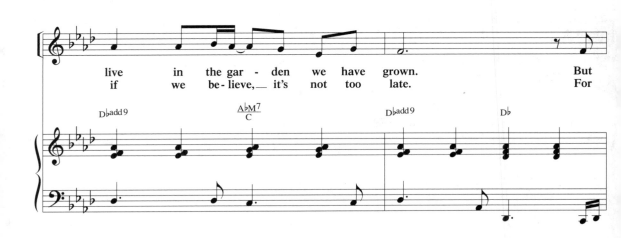

live in the gar - den we have grown. But
if we be - lieve,___ it's not too late. For

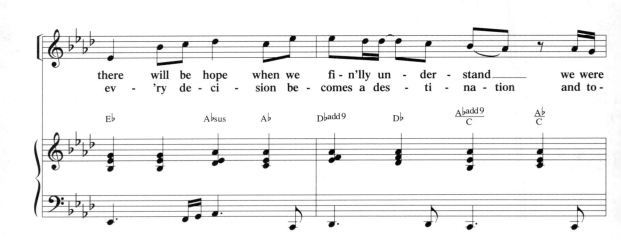

there will be hope when we fi - n'lly un - der - stand___ we were
ev - 'ry de - ci - sion be - comes a des - ti - na - tion and to -

82

84

O I Want to Know You More

S.F.

STEVE FRY
Arr. by Lloyd Larson

89

I Will Be Here

S.C.C.

STEVEN CURTIS CHAPMAN

92

95

96

Be Ye Glad

M.K.B.

MICHAEL KELLY BLANCHARD
Arr. by Lloyd Larson

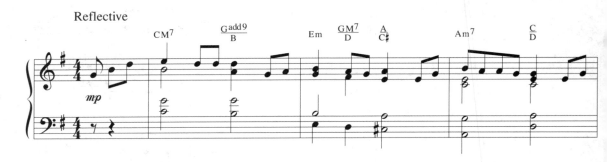

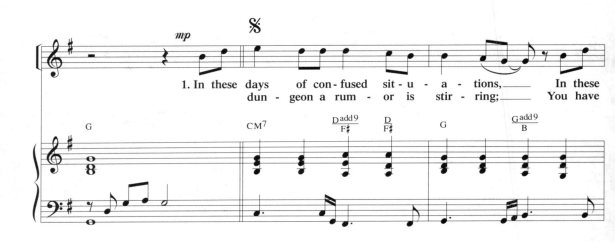

1. In these days of con - fused sit - u - a - tions,_____ In these
   dun - geon a rum - or is stir - ring;_____ You have

nights of a rest - less re - morse, When the heart and the soul of a
heard it a - gain and a - gain. Ah, but this time the cell keys– they're

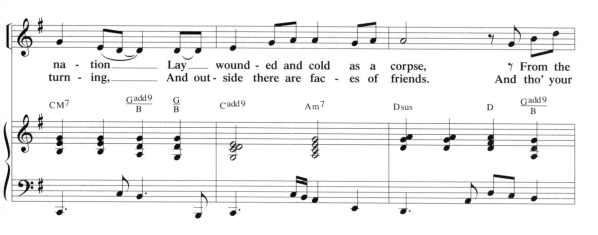

na - tion_____ Lay___ wound - ed and cold as a corpse, From the
turn - ing,_____ And out - side there are fac - es of friends. And tho' your

grave of the in - no - cent A - dam_____ Comes a song bring-ing joy to the
bod - y lay wea - ry from wast - ing,_____ And your eyes show the sor - row they've

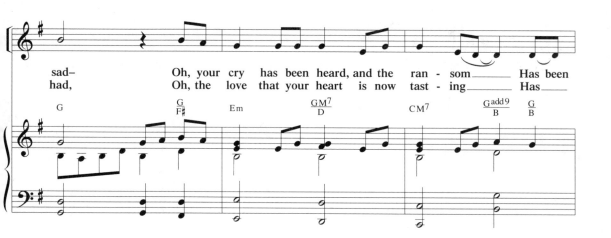

sad— Oh, your cry has been heard, and the ran - som_____ Has been
had, Oh, the love that your heart is now tast - ing_____ Has

100

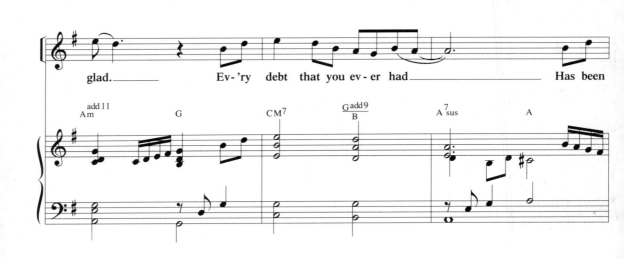

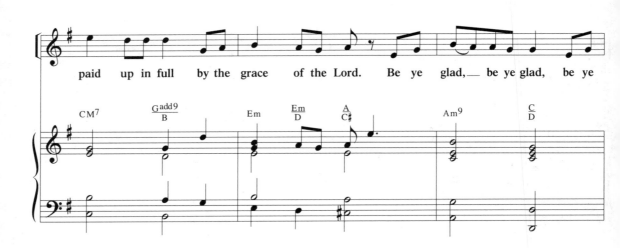

Be Strong and Take Courage

BASIL CHIASSON
Arr. by Lloyd Larson

B.C.

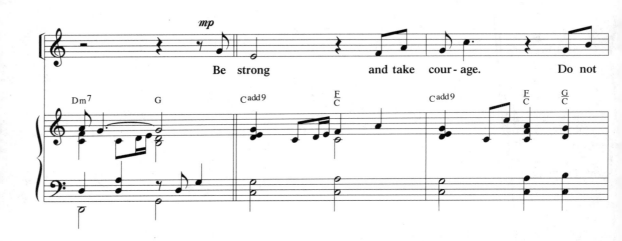

105

Deep River

Traditional Spiritual

Traditional Spiritual
Arr. by Lloyd Larson

With feeling, freely

Deep___ riv - er, my home is o - ver Jor - dan;

Deep___ riv - er, Lord, I want to cross o - ver in - to

camp - ground. Deep___ riv - er, my

home is o - ver Jor - dan; Deep

riv - er, Lord, I want to cross o - ver in - to camp - ground.

Oh, don't you want to go to that gos - pel

feast, That prom - ised land where

110

Goin' Home

WILLIAM ARMS FISHER

ANTONIN DVORAK
Arr. by Lloyd Larson

Tenderly, freely

Go - in' home, go - in' home, I'm a go - in' home;

Qui - et - like some still day, I'm just go - in' home.

Lots of folks gath - ered there– all the friends I knew.

Morn - ing star lights the way;

rest - less dream all done.

Shad - ows gone, break of day,

114

Ten Thousand Angels

R.O.

RAY OVERHOLT

118

120

Christ in Us Be Glorified

M.C.

MORRIS CHAPMAN

love be shown and His prais-es be known; Let___ Christ be glo - ri -

fied. Let___ Christ be glo - ri - fied. Let

Slightly faster, steady

Christ in___us be glo - ri - fied; Let Christ in___us be
Christ in___us be glo - ri - fied. Let Christ in___us be

122

124

126

O Lord, Most Holy
(Panis Angelicus)

C.F.

CESAR FRANCK

Expressively, freely

rit.

O Lord, most ho - ly, O Lord, most ho - ly, O lov - ing Fa - ther, we would e'er be prais - ing Thee. Help us to praise_ Thee, praise Thee and love_ Thee.

Fa - ther, Fa - ther, grant us Thy lov - ing

care; Fa - ther, Fa - ther,

grant us Thy lov - ing care;

rit.

My Jesus, I Love Thee

WILLIAM R. FEATHERSTON

DEBORAH CRISER
Arr. by Lloyd Larson

With feeling, freely

132

134

He's Been Faithful

C.C.

CAROL CYMBALA

With feeling, very freely

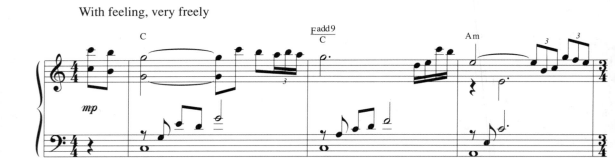

fear, thro' ev-'ry pain,_____ ev-'ry tear, There's a God who's been
way, the man-y times I could not pray, Still my God— He was

137

faith- ful to me.____ ⅞ When my strength____ was all
faith- ful to me.____ The days I spent so self- ish-

gone, when my heart____ had no song, Still in love, He's proved
ly, reach- ing out for what pleased me— E- ven then God was

faith- ful____ to me.____ Ev- 'ry word He's
faith- ful____ to me.____ Ev- 'ry time I

138

139

140

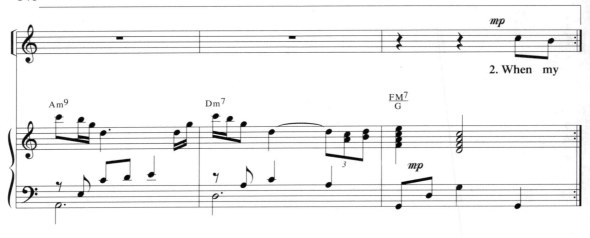

Field of Souls

W. W.

WAYNE WATSON
Arr. by Lloyd Larson

143

145

Who has la - bored best?
in si - lence on her knees

Oh, that life de-vot - ed to our God,
Be - fore the throne day af - ter day

that de-vo - tion will be blessed.
where hu - man eyes don't see.

146

It Was Enough

L.B.

LARRY BRYANT
Arr. by Lloyd Larson

Gently, yet with assurance

1. Lord, I see_____ so much in me_____
"Child, you know_____ it hurts me so_____

that I just can't get__ right–
to see you strug - gle__ on,

Things that weigh__ me down
Striv - ing to_____ be good

_ each day,_____ that steal my sleep at night.
_ e - nough_____ till all your strength is gone,

In Your Word_____ I read a - bout____ a peace I wish__ I_____
Worn out by_____ the fear that you____ will go one sin__ too_____

felt, But how can You_____ for - give me when__ I
far. But don't you know_____ that on - ly I____ could

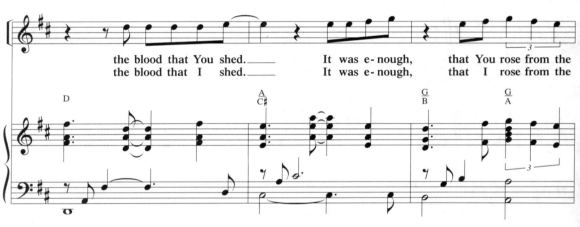

that You died____ for me.

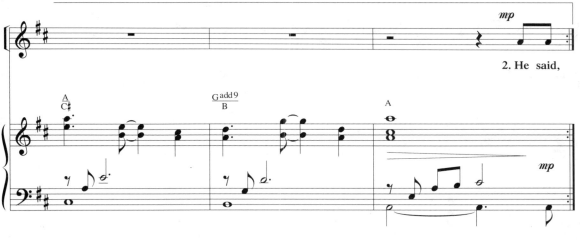

2. He said,

It was e-nough,   the life that You gave.____   It was e-nough,

Beyond What I Can See

L.H., M.K., and D.W.

LARNELLE HARRIS, MAK KAYLOR, and DARRYL WILLIAMS
Arr. by Lloyd Larson

With assurance

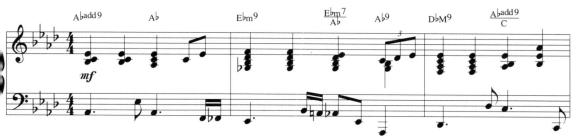

1. My God is faith-ful,
wor - thy.

for not one
If not an -

prom - ise He_____ has made_ has gone un - ful - filled,
oth - er bless - ing came_ I'd still give Him praise

all ac -
all the

154

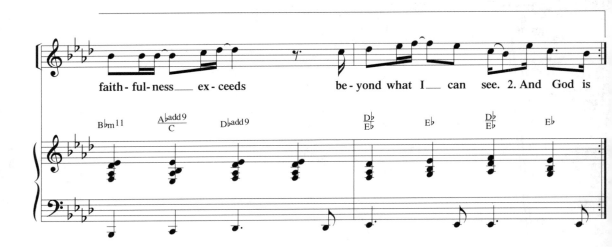

156

158

Thanks

C.McG.

CARROLL McGRUDER
Arr. by Lloyd Larson

I am so blessed; my soul is at rest. O

Lord,_____ I give You thanks._____

I'm gon-na give You_

thank You, Lord,_____ for the strength You give_____ to_____ sim - ply car - ry
give You thanks_____ this_____ mo - ment,_____ and I will con - tin - ual-

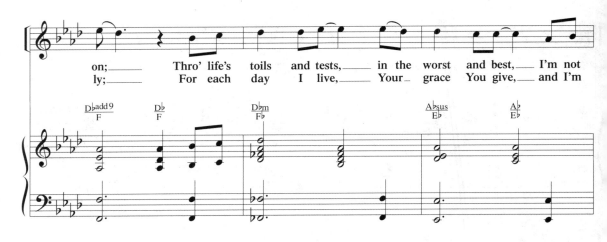

on;_____ Thro' life's toils and tests,____ in the worst and best,____ I'm not
ly;_____ For each day I live,____ Your__ grace You give,____ and I'm

ev - er left____ a - lone.____ You are al - ways right____ be -
blessed a - bun - dant - ly.____ I__ can't for - get____ that

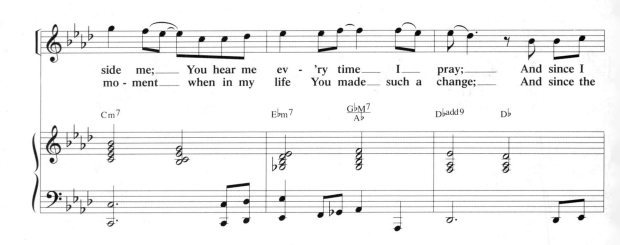

side me;____ You hear me ev - 'ry time__ I__ pray;____ And since I
mo - ment____ when in my life You made__ such a change;____ And since the

A Name I Highly Treasure

O.C.E.

OSCAR C. ELIASON
Arr. by Lloyd Larson

1. I've learned to know a name I high-ly trea-sure. O how it
glad - ness to a soul in sor - row. It makes life's

thrills my spir - it through and through! O pre - cious
shad - ows and its clouds de - part; Brings strength in

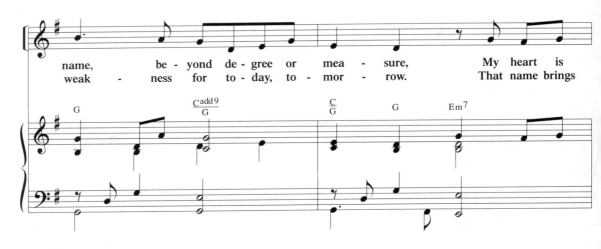

name, be - yond de - gree or mea - sure, My heart is
weak - ness for to - day, to - mor - row. That name brings

stirred when - e'er I think of You! 2. That name brings
heal - ing to an ach - ing

heart. My heart is stirred when - e'er I think of

168

All in the Name of Jesus

S.R.A.

STEPHEN R. ADAMS
Arr. by Lloyd Larson

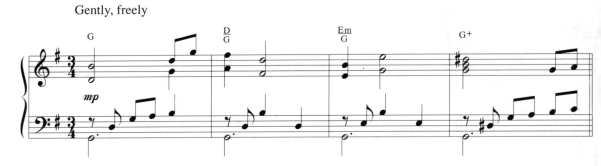

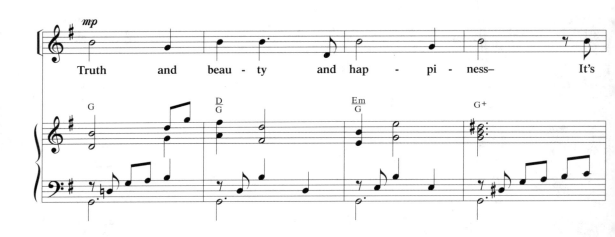

Truth and beau-ty and hap-pi-ness— It's

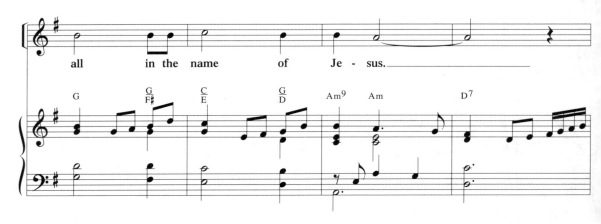

all in the name of Je-sus.

172

173

174

This Too Shall Pass

T.L. and C.H.

TY LACY and CONNIE HARRINGTON
Arr. by Lloyd Larson

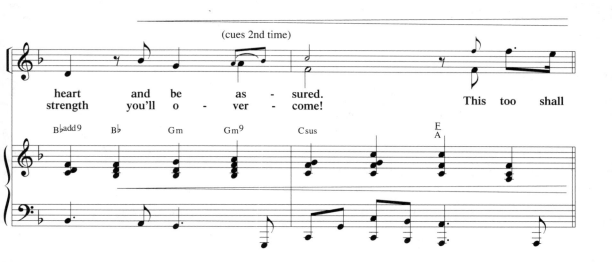

178

180

I Can Be Glad

LARNELLE HARRIS
Arr. by Lloyd Larson

L. H.

Driving, with energy

I can be glad, for my hope is in the Lord, 'Cause He gives a con-fi-dence that this

183

184

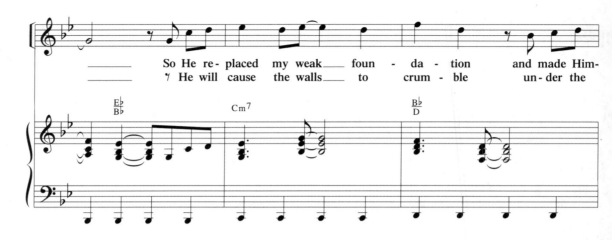

way. That's why I'm glad, for my

hope is in the Lord, 'Cause He gives a con - fi - dence

that this world does-n't know. He's the Lord of all cre -

I Will Bring You Home

M.C. (based on Zephaniah 3:20)

MICHAEL CARD
Arr. by Lloyd Larson

Though you are home-less, though you're a-lone, I will be your Home. What-

190

Mercy Saw Me

G.D. and B.D.

GERON and BECKY DAVIS
Arr. by Lloyd Larson

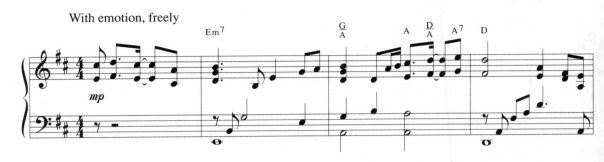

1. The years had left scars, the scars had left pain.
done, you can't go too far

How could He recognize me?
That His eyes of mercy

I was-n't the same._____ I knew I__ should
can't see where you are._____ He loves you__ too

pay and I knew the price,
much to leave you a - lone;

For jus-tice and law_____ de-mand-ed__ my
You're flesh of His flesh_____ and bone of__ His

194

196

198

How Great the Love

D.W.

DAN WHITTEMORE
Arr. by Lloyd Larson

1. How great the love,_____ how great the love___ of the Fa-
2. Love has a name;_____ love has a name,__ and it's Je-

- ther,
- sus.

Call-ing us all,_____
He took a-way,_____

(simile)

call - ing us all_____ His own,_____
He took a - way_____ my sin._____

A   D   D

Chil - dren of God,_____ born not of flesh___ but of Spir - it.
Down in the grave_____ went all that en - slaved___ and con - demned___ me.

D   G   D

And what shall be_____ in time,   I know that He will make
I con - fess Christ___ as Lord;   I prayed and He en - tered

D   A   A7

202

203

204

Desire of My Heart

BEVERLY DARNALL

JEFF SLAUGHTER
Arr. by Lloyd Larson

Gently, not too fast

208

I Surrender All

D.M. and R.H.

DAVID MOFFITT and REGIE HAMM
Arr. by Lloyd Larson

Steady, not too fast

1. I have wres - tled in___ the dark - ness of this
   source of my___ am - bi - tion is the

lone - ly pil - grim land, Rais - ing strong and might - y for - tress - es___ that
trea - sure I___ ob - tain, If I mea - sure my___ suc - cess - es on___ a

I a - lone___ com - mand. But these cas - tles I've___ con - struct - ed by the
scale of earth - ly gain; If the fo - cus of___ my vis - ion is the

strength of my_ own hand   Are just tem - po - rar - y king - doms   on foun-
sta - tus I_ at - tain,   My ac - com - plish - ments_ are worth - less   and my

da - tions made_ of sand.   In the mid - dle of_ the bat - tle,   I be-
ef - forts are_ in vain.   So I lay a - side_ these tro - phies   to pur-

lieve I've fin - 'lly found   I'll nev - er know the thrill_ of vic - t'ry 'til_ I'm
sue a high - er crown,   And should You choose some - how_ to use the life_ I_

212

214

Not Too Far from Here

T.L. and S.S.

TY LACY and STEVE SILER
Arr. by Lloyd Larson

With gentle motion

1. Some-bod-y's down ____ to their ____ last dime; Some-bod-y's run-
2. Some-bod-y's trou - bled and ____ con - fused; Some-bod-y's got noth-

And I may_____ not know____ their____ name, But I'm pray-
It may be_____ a stran - ger's____ face, But I'm pray-

- in' just____ the same_____ That You'll use_____ me, Lord,_____ to
- ing for____ Your grace_____ To move_____ in me_____ and

wipe a - way____ a tear, 'Cause some-bod - y's cry-
take a - way____ the fear, 'Cause some-bod - y's hurt-

220

It's Still the Cross

N.B., M.H., L.G., & B.M.

NILES BOROP, MIKE HARLAND,
LUKE GARRETT, & BUDDY MULLINS
Arr. by Lloyd Larson

1. It's not con-ser-va-tive___ or lib-er-al, how-
strat-e-gize___ and im-ple-ment our

ev-er they're___ de-fined;
stanc-es and___ de-crees;
It's not a-bout in-ter-pre-ta-tions___ or the
We can con-trol our in-sti-tu-tions, ap-

judg-ments of the mind.___
prove and grant de-grees.___
It's the op-po-site___ of pol-i-tics,___
But the world is out___ there watch-ing, and

224

sets the cap - tive free. It's still the name, the name of

Je - sus that has pow'r to save the lost. It's still the

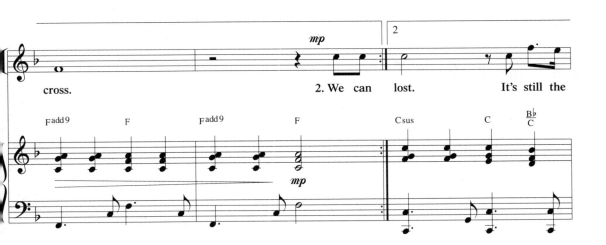

cross. 2. We can lost. It's still the

Here We Stand

KEN BIBLE

TOM FETTKE
Arr. by Lloyd Larson

232

Look unto Jesus

D.A. and N.A. (based on Hebrews 12)

DENNIS and NAN ALLEN
Arr. by Lloyd Larson

With strength and conviction

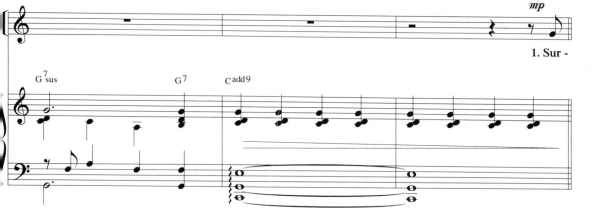

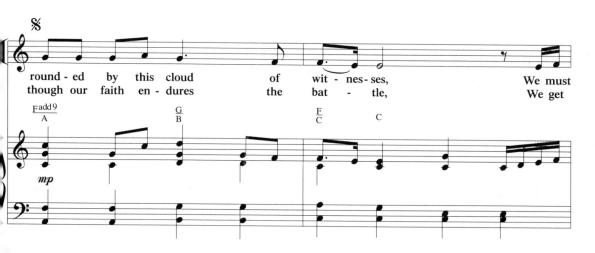

235

Audience of One

G.F.

GREG FERGUSON
Arr. by Lloyd Larson

239

240

242

Beyond the Open Door

S. C.

SHAWN CRAIG
Arr. by Lloyd Larson

1. In the things___ fa - mil - iar you find se - cu - ri - ty,___
2. Hear the Spir - it call - ing to wake the liv - ing dead,

___ Re - sist - ing all___ the chang - es___ the
___ To reach the hud - dled mass - es___ who cry

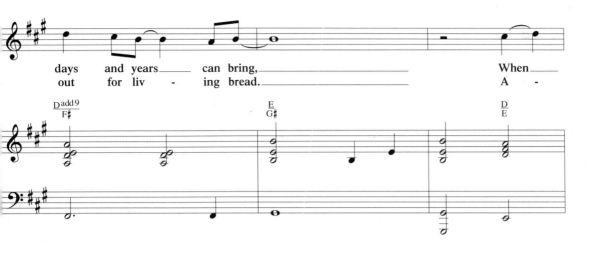

days and years___ can bring,_____ When___
out for liv - ing bread._____ A -

God de - cides__ to lead__ you_____ 𝄽 through an o - pen door,
rise, O might - y ar - my,_____ take up thy shield__ and sword,

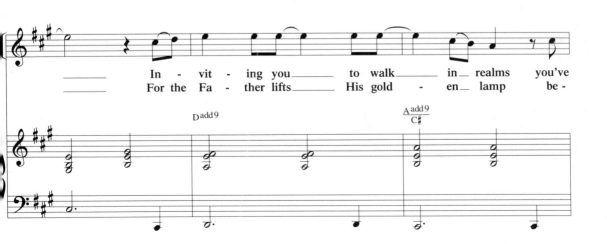

_____ In - vit - ing you_____ to walk_____ in__ realms you've
_____ For the Fa - ther lifts_____ His gold - en lamp be -

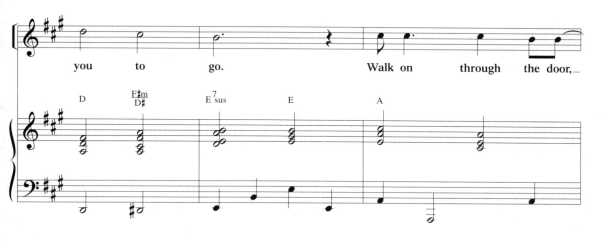

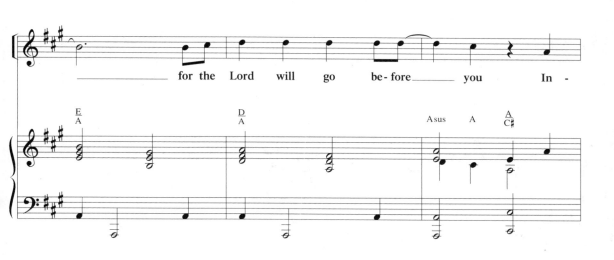

Hear the Spir - it call - ing you to go.

Walk on through the door,_____ for the Lord will go be-fore

____ you In - to a great-er pow - er_____ you've

250

"Where He Leads Me" (Blandy - Norris)

fol - low_____ In - to a great - er pow - er_____

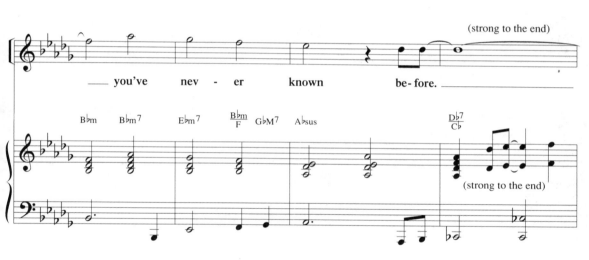

_____ you've nev - er known be - fore. _____

We Are Waiting on You

K.N. and C.S.

KIM NOBLITT and CHRIS SPRINGER
Arr. by Lloyd Larson

Gently, freely

254

Wonderful Words of Life

P.P.B.

PHILIP P. BLISS
Arr. by Lloyd Larson

Gently flowing

1. Sing them o - ver a - gain to me—
2. Christ, the bless - ed One, gives to all

Won-der - ful words of life!
Won-der - ful words of life!

Let me more of their
Sin - ner, list to the

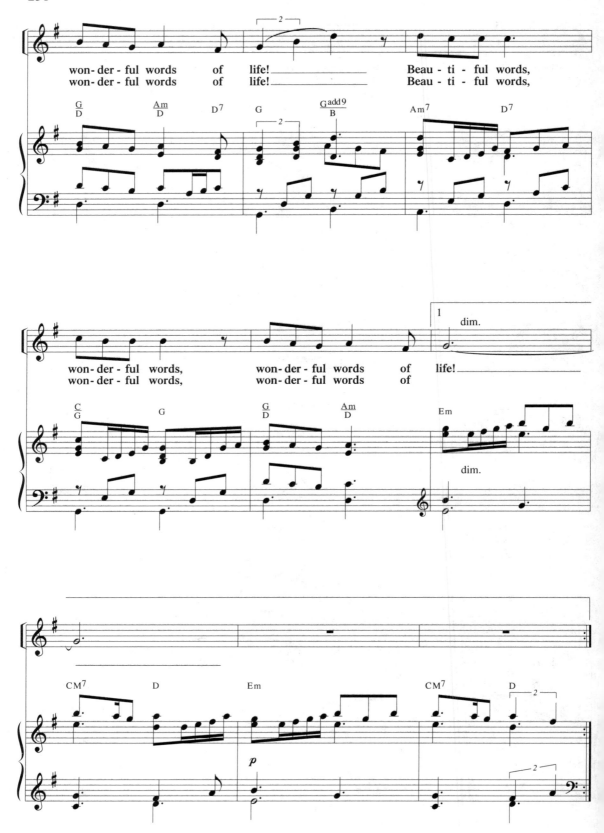

score
259

Father, Forgive

KEN BIBLE

STEVEN V. TAYLOR
Arr. by Lloyd Larson

1. When blown by the winds of my weak - ness, On the
   shame in my soul weighs so heav - y That I

sea of my self - cen-tered ways, The dark-ness of guilt and de-spair
wres-tle to win my re - lease; But Cal-va - ry whis - pers com-pas-

set - tles in,_____ And I long for the light_____ of Your face._____
sion and love_____ And for - give - ness and free - dom and peace._____

Fa - ther, for - give.   O - pen,   I

come,_____   De - pend - ing on_____ Your pres - ence_____ and

thirst - ing for__ Your love.__ Fa - ther, for -

give. Trust - ing, I come.__

In - vit - ed by__ Your mer - cy,__ I rest in You__ a -

Near to the Heart of God

C.B.McA.

CLELAND B. McAFEE
Arr. by Lloyd Larson

1. There is a place of qui - et rest,
is a place of com - fort sweet,

near to the heart of God;
near to the heart of God;

A place where sin can -
A place where we our

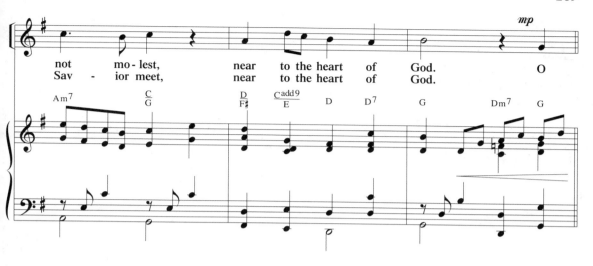

not mo - lest, near to the heart of God. O
Sav - ior meet, near to the heart of God.

Je - sus, blest Re - deem - er, sent from the heart of

God, Hold us, who wait be - fore Thee,

272

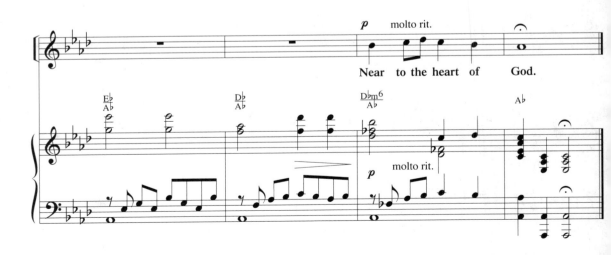

Beneath His Father's Heaven

T. L. and D. L.

TY LACY and DWIGHT LILES
Arr. by Lloyd Larson

did not un-der-stand__ His on-ly pur-pose__ was to save the
truth__ and of grace. The glo-ry of the__ Fa-ther shin-ing

fall - en soul of man. Be -
bright up - on His face.

neath His Fa-ther's heav - en, hope was

born _____ one si - lent night. Be -

neath His Fa-ther's heav - en, a ba - by

brought _____ the truth to life. A ba - by

A Quiet Joy

KEITH FERGUSON

BRUCE GREER
Arr. by Lloyd Larson

1. The shin - ing light, the shep - herd's flight, the
proph - et's prayer, a son to bear, a
Fa - ther's plan be - came a man with

an - gel's song. No crown to wear, no
sa - cred trust. A prom - ise made, a
us to dwell. God's on - ly Son, the

great fan - fare, no swell - ing throng._____ A
peo - ple saved, God is with us._____ A
Ho - ly One, Em - man - u - el._____ A

C/G   Em   Bm/D

barn in - stead, a man - ger bed, a ba - by boy._____
moth - er's tears, a fa - ther's fears did not de - stroy_____
prom - ised sign, a King di - vine, a ba - by boy._____

C   G/B   Am11   C/G   F

3rd time to Coda ⊕

A hum - ble place to see His face, a
Their sim - ple faith, their gen - tle grace, their
The Prince of Peace, our soul's re - lease, our

C6/D   D/G   C/G

282

283

Our God Is with Us

S.C.C. and M.W.S.

STEVEN CURTIS CHAPMAN and MICHAEL W. SMITH
Arr. by Lloyd Larson

With steady motion

1. One of us_____ is cry-in' as our
   spoke with proph-ets' voic-es and_____

hopes and dreams are led a-way_____ in chains, And we're
showed Him-self_____ in a cloud_____ of fire, But no

287

288

290

Gesú Bambino

FREDERICK H. MARTENS

PIETRO A. YON

Gently, freely, with expression

an - gels sang,___ the shep-herds sang,___ the grate - ful earth___ re - joiced,___
ev - 'ry voice___ ac - claim His name, the grate - ful cho - rus swell.___

And at___ His bless - ed birth the stars their ex - al - ta - tion
From par - a - dise___ to earth He came that we___ with Him might

voiced.___ O come, let us a -
dwell.___

Expressively, not too slow

dore Him. O come, let us a -

dore__ Him, Christ_ the Lord.   O   come,_____   O

come,_____   O   come,__ let us____ a -

dore_____ Him.   Let   us   a -

dore_____ Him,   Christ_____ the Lord._____

All Is Well

W.K. and M.W.S.

WAYNE KIRKPATRICK and MICHAEL W. SMITH
Arr. by Lloyd Larson

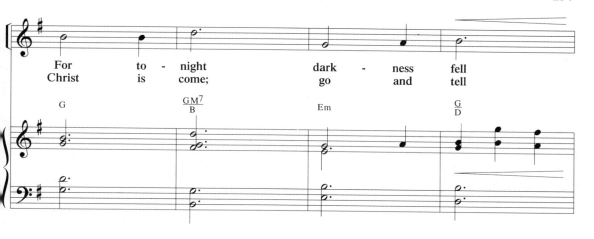

298

300

TOPICAL INDEX

ALPHABETICAL INDEX